Super-Duper Series

Exciting Earth!

by Annalisa McMorrow
illustrated by Marilynn G. Barr

Publisher: Roberta Suid
Design & Production: Scott McMorrow
Cover Design: David Hale
Cover Art: Mike Artell

Also in the Super-Duper series: *Incredible Insects!* (MM 2018),
Spectacular Space! (MM 2019), *Outstanding Oceans!* (MM 2020),
Wacky Weather! (MM 2057), *Peculiar Plants!* (MM 2058), *Amazing Animals!* (MM 2059),
Leapin' Lizards! (MM 2100), *Terrific Transportation!* (MM 2102),
and *Marvelous Money!* (MM 2103)

P.O. Box 1680
Palo Alto, CA 94302

E-mail us at: MMBooks@aol.com
Visit our Web site: www.mondaymorningbooks.com
Call us at: 1-800-255-6049

ISBN 1-57612-111-9

Printed in the United States of America
987654321

Contents

20,000 feet

17,500 feet

Snow and ice all year

15,500 feet

Alpine meadows

12,500 feet

Cone-bearing evergreens

10,000 feet

Leaf-shedding trees

7,500 feet

Tropical forest

5,000 feet

2,500 feet

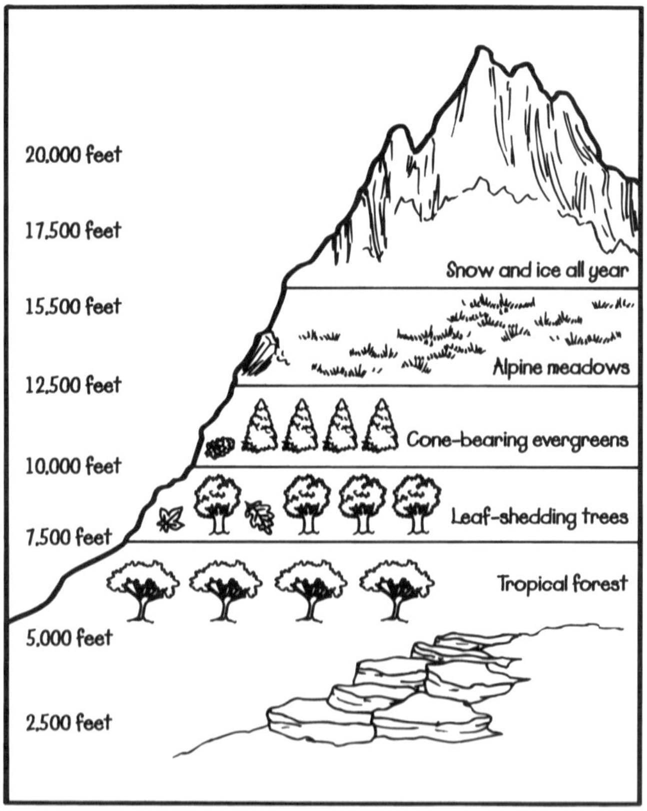

Introduction: Why Earth?

Deserts, rain forests, islands, mountains, caverns, and canyons—the Earth is home to a wide variety of environments. And with earthquakes, volcanoes, and avalanches, there is always something going on! Through the geology and geography activities in this book, your students will learn about the fascinating world around them while practicing writing, reading, research, performance, and speaking skills. They'll interview an explorer, create Earth ABC books, make their own maps, and much more. Most of the activities can be simplified for younger students or extended for upper grades.

Exciting Earth! is divided into four parts and a resource section. Through a variety of activities, **Hands-On Discoveries** will help answer questions such as "What's under the Earth's crust?" and "What is the difference between a stalactite and a stalagmite?" Reproducible sheets with a special globe icon have directions written specifically for the children. This section also features art activities, such as "Naming Jewels" in which the children can explore their creativity.

Nonfiction Book Links feature speaking, writing, and reporting activities based on nonfiction resources. Many activities are accompanied by helpful handouts, which will lead the children through the research procedure. When research is required, you have the option of letting children look for the facts needed in your classroom or school or local library, or on the Internet. Or use the "Super-Duper Fact Cards" located in the resource section at the back of this book. These cards list information for 16 Earth-related subjects. You can duplicate the cards onto neon-colored paper, laminate, and cut them out. Then store the cards in a box for children to choose from when doing their research. These cards also provide an opportunity for younger children to participate in research projects. The information is available to them on easy-to-read cards.

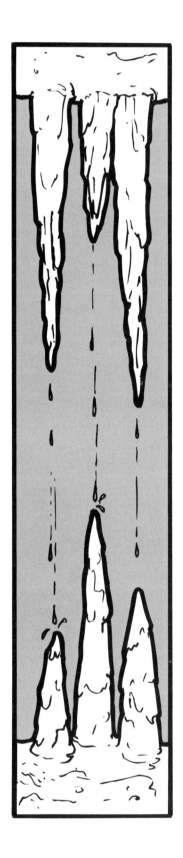

The **Fiction Book Links** section uses chapter books and storybooks to introduce information about the Earth. This section's activities, projects, and language extensions help children connect with the world around them. Each "Link" also includes a tongue twister. Challenge children to create their own twisters from the Earth facts and words they've learned. Also included in this section are decorating suggestions (called "setting the stage") for each particular book. Creating a book-friendly environment in the classroom will encourage children to read on their own for fun.

It's Show Time! presents new songs sung to old tunes. The songs can be duplicated and given to the children to learn. If you want to hold a performance, write each performer's name on the reproducible program page and distribute the copies to your audience. Consider having the children make costumes to go with the songs.

Three sections in this book end with a "Super-Duper Project," an activity that uses the information children have learned in the unit. A choral performance is one possible "Super-Duper" ending for the "It's Show Time!" section.

This unit is a perfect time to explore any environment resources that are available in your area. For instance, consider a field trip to a famous cave or cavern, if your school is near one.

All About Earth

Planet Earth is the third planet from the sun. It has four layers: the inner core, the outer core, the mantle, and the crust.

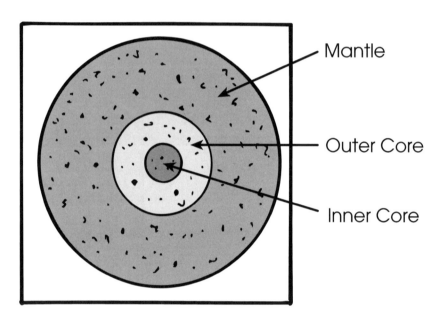

Scientists believe that Earth's inner core is made of solid iron and nickel. The inner core is hot—about 50 times as hot as boiling water.

The outer core surrounds the inner core. Scientists believe that the outer core is also made of iron and nickel, but the outer core is hot liquid instead of hot solid.

The mantle is around the outer core. It is mostly solid, but some of the outer mantle is made of melted rock.

The crust is outside of the mantle. The crust is made of rock and soil. It is the thinnest layer of the Earth.

All About Earth

The Earth's crust has two parts. One part is under the ocean. This is called the oceanic crust. It makes up the ocean floor. The other part is called the continental crust. Oceanic crust that runs under the continental crust forms the land above sea level.

The crust is divided into pieces called plates. There are seven major plates and many smaller plates. The plates curve to fit Earth's shape. They are made of crust and outer mantle. The plates move because they float on top of the partially melted rock that makes up the mantle. Under the oceans, the plates are about 40 miles (64 km) thick. Under the continents, they are about 60 miles (96 km) thick.

Learning the Order

The Earth is the third planet from the sun. This activity will help the children remember the order of the planets.

Materials:
Planetary Patterns (p. 9), crayons or markers, scissors, construction paper, glue, pens or pencils

Directions:
1. Duplicate a copy of the Planetary Patterns for each child.
2. Have the children cut out the planets and color them as desired.
3. Explain that the children will be learning the order of the planets. Teach the children the correct order: Mercury, Venus, Earth, Mars, Jupiter, Saturn, Uranus, Neptune, Pluto. Then tell them the order and have them glue the planets in place on a sheet of construction paper.
4. Explain the concept of a mnemonic. A mnemonic is a device that helps people remember something. Share a planetary mnemonic with the children. For instance, one way to remember the order of the planets is:
Most Very Exciting Monsters Jump Softly Upon Nick's Piano.
5. Have the children work to come up with their own mnemonics. They can write them under the planets on their sheets of construction paper.
6. Give each child a chance to share his or her mnemonic with the class.
7. Post the pictures and mnemonics on a "We're Number Three!" bulletin board.

Option:
• Have the children make up other mnemonic devices throughout the year.

Planetary Patterns

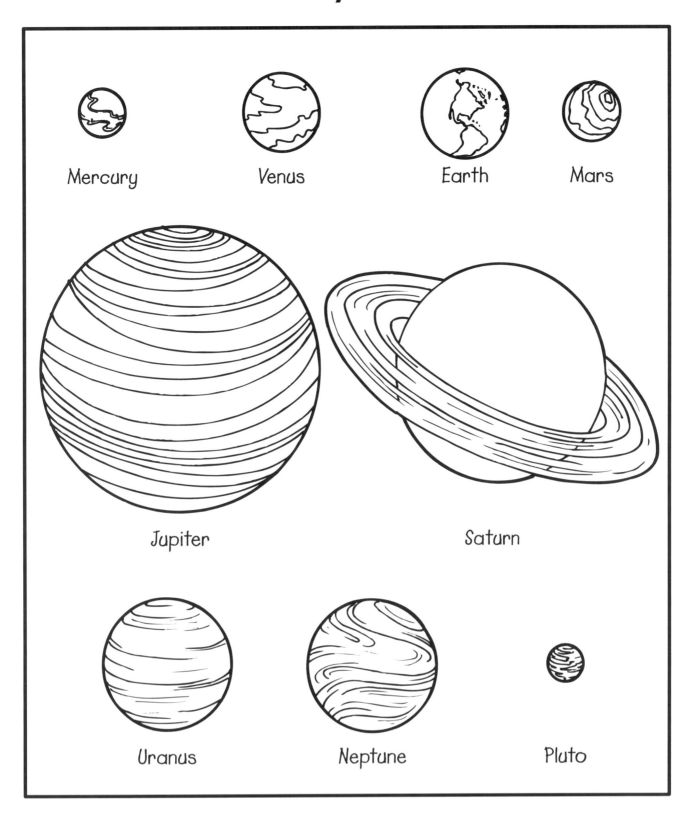

Mercury

Venus

Earth

Mars

Jupiter

Saturn

Uranus

Neptune

Pluto

Jigsaw Continents

Scientists believe that about 200 million years ago, there was one giant continent where the Atlantic Ocean is today. This continent is called Pangaea, meaning "all lands." About 1,890 million years ago, Pangaea began to break apart. Eventually, the giant continent became the continents we have today.

Materials:
Pangaea Puzzle (p. 11), scissors, envelopes (one per child)

Directions:
1. Duplicate a copy of the puzzle for each child.
2. Explain the theory of Pangaea. Nobody can prove that this theory is correct. However, scientists believe that the bulge of Africa fits with the shape of the coast of North America. The clues to Pangaea are found in today's maps.
3. Have the children cut apart the puzzle pieces and then put them together.
4. Give each child an envelope to use to store his or her puzzle pieces.

Options:
• Children can decorate their puzzles using crayons or markers.
• This activity is the perfect opportunity to familiarize students with the names of the continents.

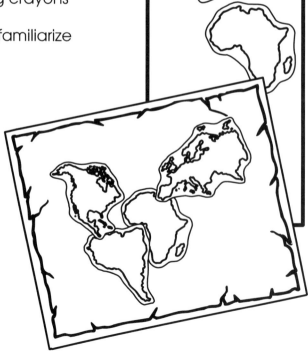

Pangaea Puzzle

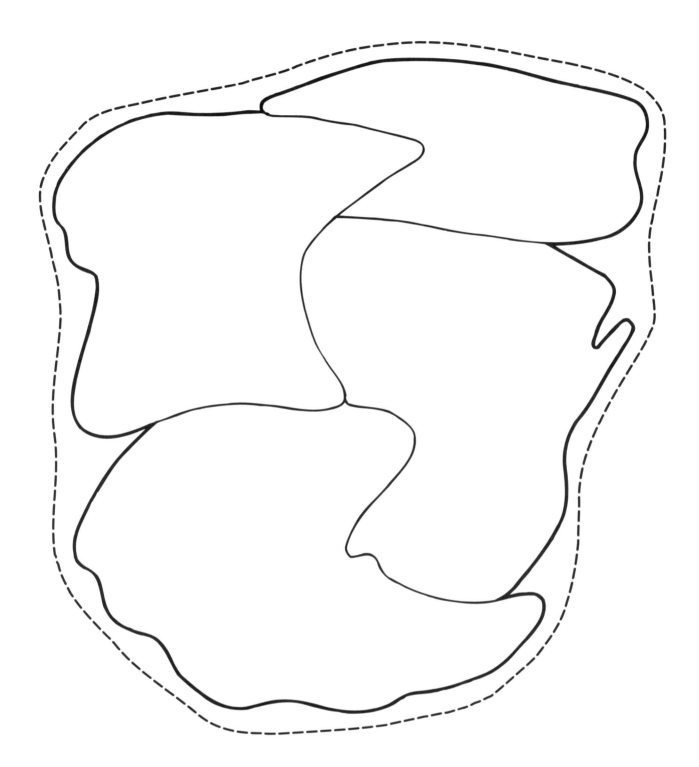

Eating the Earth

The Earth is composed of four layers. The first is a solid ball, surrounded by an outer liquid core, surrounded by the mantle, and then by the crust.

Materials:
All About Earth (p. 6), apples or other thin-skinned fruits (one for each group of four children), knife (for adult use only), plates, napkins

Directions:
1. Duplicate a copy of the All About Earth handout for each child.
2. Have the children read the handout.
3. Explain that the Earth is made of four levels. Have the children look at the sheet to name the different levels. Point out that three of the levels are far thicker than the fourth.
4. Divide the children into groups of four and give each group an apple.
5. Explain that the apple represents the Earth. If Earth were the size of an apple, its fourth level—the crust—would be about as thin as the skin on an apple!
6. Cut the apple into sections so that the children can see exactly how thin the skin of an apple is.
7. Serve the apple sections as a snack.

Thin-skinned fruits to serve:
• In season, choose pears, peaches, or nectarines.

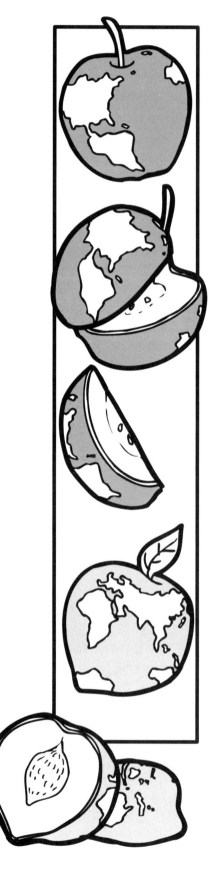

Molten Molasses

This sticky activity will reinforce how slowly the Earth's mantle moves beneath the crust. Consider placing newspaper under the workstations before passing out the molasses.

Materials:
All About Earth (p. 7), molasses, clear plastic cups (two per group), crackers

Directions:
1. Duplicate the All About Earth handout for the children to read.
2. Explain that the third layer of the Earth is mostly solid. However, part of it is made of melted rock. This part moves slowly, like molasses.
3. Divide the children into small groups. Give each group a cup of molasses.
4. Have the children demonstrate how slowly the mantle moves by pouring a cup of molasses from one container to another.
5. Have the children place pieces of crackers on top of the molasses mantle to show how the plates float on top of the mantle.

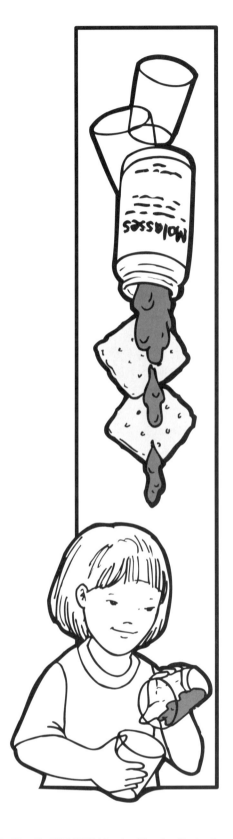

A Hands-on Earthquake

In ancient Greece, people thought earthquakes were caused by the dead fighting. Japanese legend claimed that earthquakes came when the great spider that carried the earth on its back moved. In Siberia, people believed that earthquakes happened when the giant dog named Kasei shook snow off its back.

Materials:
"What Makes an Earthquake?" Hands-on Handout (p. 15)

Directions:
1. Duplicate a copy of the "What Makes an Earthquake?" Hands-on Handout for each child. Discuss what makes an earthquake happen.
2. Have the children imagine what it might have been like to live through an earthquake in ancient times. People didn't know why earthquakes happened, which made them even more frightening. Describe some of the ancient people's beliefs in earthquake causes, listed above.
3. Have the children do the following experiment. They should hold their hands out with the palms up. Then they should press their hands together as hard as they can. This represents the plates pressing against each other. Maintaining pressure, they should try to slide one hand up along the other. It should be difficult for them to do. Have the children keep trying to slide one hand along the other until it breaks free. Explain that the sudden burst of energy they feel is similar to the burst of energy that occurs when one of Earth's plates breaks free. The burst of energy causes an earthquake.

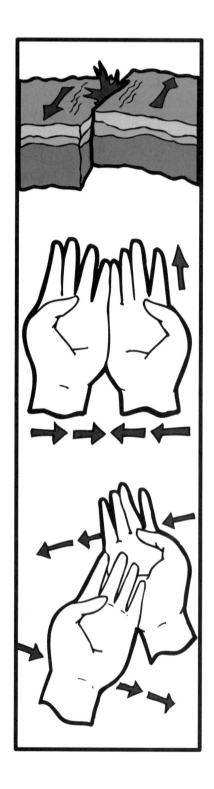

What Makes an Earthquake?

The surface of the Earth is broken up into seven major plates. Each one is thousands of miles (km) wide and thousands of miles (km) across. The plates are made of rock.

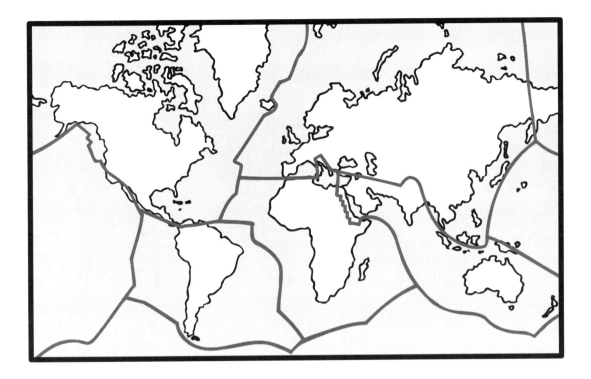

The plates fit together tightly. The plates move all the time. Usually, they move small distances. They move so slowly that nobody sees them or feels them. When the plates move, they can press together and become locked. When this happens, neither plate can slide past the other. Pressure builds between the plates. When one of the plates finally breaks free, it can make the Earth shake and tremble. This is an earthquake.

Exciting Earth! © 2000 Monday Morning Books, Inc.

Outsmarting an Earthquake

Materials:
Milk cartons and assorted cardboard boxes, tape, glue, large sheet of cardboard, construction paper, tag board, file folders, tempera paint, paintbrushes, shallow tins for paint, scissors

Directions:
1. Explain that the children will be creating a miniature town and then seeing how well the buildings hold up in a quake.
2. Provide different-sized boxes for the children to use to make buildings. All buildings should be more than one story, and made from two or more boxes.
3. Let the children paint their buildings.
4. Children can use construction paper, tag board, old file folders, and other items to create their town.
5. Cut a large sheet of cardboard into two jagged pieces, and set the pieces back together. Then have the children set their buildings on the cardboard base.
6. Once the town is set up, have the children take hold of the two parts of the cardboard base and push them against each other. They should start slowly and observe what happens to their town. Then have the children jerk the cardboard so that the plates come apart.
7. Ask the children questions about the experiment, such as "How did the buildings handle the earthquake?" and "What could be done to make the buildings stronger?"

Note:
Use the "Earthquake Awareness Quiz" handout (p. 17) to discuss earthquake preparedness with your students.

Book Link:
• *Francis the Earthquake Dog* by Judith Ross Enderle and Stephanie Gordon Tessler, (Chronicle, 1996).

Earthquake Awareness Quiz

Match the lettered statements with the numbered answers.

A. If you are inside when an earthquake happens...

_____

B. If you are outdoors...

_____

C. If you are in a high-rise building...

_____

D. If you are in a crowded public area...

_____

1. Move away from trees, buildings, power lines, and walls.

2. Move away from windows. Do not ride in an elevator.

3. Stay calm. Groups of people can panic, so do not run for the doors. Move away from any items that might fall.

4. Climb under a sturdy table or desk, or stand in a corner or a doorway.

Answers: A4, B1, C2, D3

Exciting Earth! © 2000 Monday Morning Books, Inc.

Super Speleothems

Speleothems are decorations found in caves. They are growths that occur over years, stone shapes that sprout from cave ceilings and floors. Sometimes they grow in lava-tube caves, sea caves, and sandstone caves. However, they are most often found in limestone caves.

Materials:
"Stalactites & Stalagmites" Hands-on Handout (p. 19), shoe boxes (one per child), clay, glue, pictures of stalactites and stalagmites (see **Earth Resources**)

Directions:
1. Duplicate a copy of the "Stalactites & Stalagmites" Hands-on Handout for each child.
2. Have the children study the handouts.
3. Give each child a shoe box.
4. Explain that the children will be making their own versions of stalactites and stalagmites using the shoe boxes as caves and the clay to form the speleothems.
5. Once the children have finished decorating their caves, display the caves on a table where other classes can see them.

Option:
• Display books about caves near the cave dioramas.

Mnemonic:
Stala**c**tites grow down from the **c**eiling.
Stala**g**mites grow up from the **g**round.

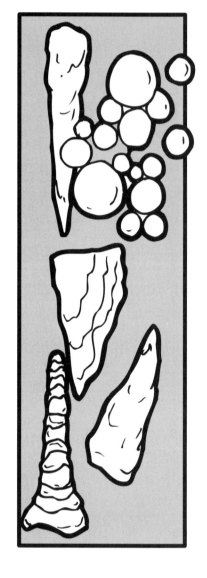

Stalactites & Stalagmites

Stalactites and stalagmites are both speleothems (SPEE-lee-oh-thems). Speleothems are growths found in caves.

Stalactites and stalagmites are rock formations created from dripping water that holds dissolved minerals.

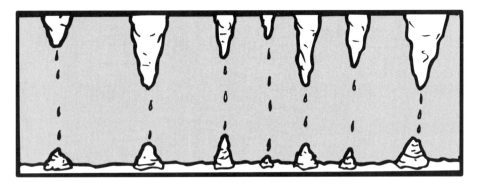

Other speleothems include cave decorations called cave popcorn, gypsum flowers, cave pearls, and moon milk. They can all be found in limestone caves.

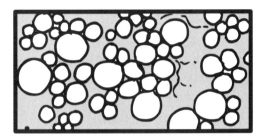

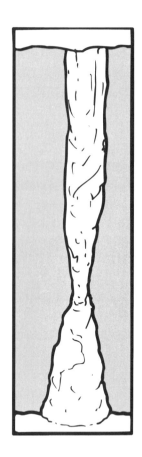

New kinds of speleothems are still being discovered!

Mountains from Molehills

Mountain ranges or chains exist on every continent. Have the children name any mountains they are familiar with before beginning this activity. Some well-known mountain chains include the Sierra Nevada and the Rockies in North America and Europe's Alps.

Materials:
Paper, pens or pencils, clay, paper plates (one per child), pictures of mountains (see **Earth Resources**)

Directions:
1. Discuss the following phrase: He or she "made a mountain out of a molehill" with the children. Have the children give examples of what this phrase means to them.
2. Give each child a ball of clay and a paper plate. Have the children create mountains on the plates using the clay. They can replicate famous mountains, such as Mt. Everest, or create their own special mountains.
3. Have the children look at their mountains and come up with new phrases. They should incorporate mountain information in their phrases. For instance, instead of "making mountains from molehills," they might say, "that problem was as big as Everest."
4. Have the children write down their new sayings and tape them to the plates.
5. Display the mountains and the mountain sayings on a table where other classes can observe them.

Option:
• Duplicate a copy of the "Marvelous Mountains" Hands-on Handout (p. 21) for the children to observe before making their mountains. They can choose to replicate different mountain shapes.

Marvelous Mountains

My Map

Reading a map is an important ability to master. In this activity, the children will make their own maps, then exchange them with partners to practice their map-reading skills.

Materials:
Maps, atlases, globes, construction paper, crayons or markers

Directions:
1. If possible, bring a local map into the classroom. Have the children try to locate their school, or street, or any parks they are familiar with.
2. Give each child a sheet of construction paper. Explain that the children will be making maps of an area they know well. Assign each child to map an area of the school: the library, your classroom, the playground, the cafeteria, and so on.
3. Once the children draw their maps, have them switch their maps with partners. Let the partners try to read the maps. Do they recognize the areas described on the maps?
4. Post the maps around the school for other students to enjoy, or use them to help parents find their way around the school on open house nights.

Option:
• Children can also try to map the neighborhood where they live, the area around their school, or a park where they play. Encourage the children to choose a small area to map.

Drawing on the Wall

About 15,000 years ago, cave dwellers in France and Spain painted animals on caves. Cave artists used chalk, clays, earth, and burnt woods to draw with. Most of the time, children are discouraged from drawing or painting on walls. This activity will allow them to explore their creative side as they pretend to be ancient cave dwellers.

Materials:
Large sheet of butcher paper, colored chalk (blue, red, orange, yellow, brown, white, and other colors)

Directions:
1. Explain that the children will be pretending to be early artists painting and drawing on a cave. Early painters were able to create a variety of colors by crushing rocks and mixing the powders with animal fats. They painted pictures of animals such as bison, deer, cows, and horses.
2. Spread the butcher paper on a flat surface.
3. Provide a variety of colored chalks for the children to use in their cave drawings. They can try to replicate the works of ancient artists, focusing on the types of animals the Cro-Magnon painters illustrated.
4. Post the completed mural near a display of cave-related resources.

Options:
• Hair spray is a great fixative for chalk!
• If possible, show the children pictures of ancient cave paintings. See **Earth Resources** for books.
• Let the children draw cave pictures on a chalkboard instead of butcher paper.

Exciting Earth! © 2000 Monday Morning Books, Inc.

Naming Jewels

The Earth is filled with an assortment of gems and jewels. Throughout history, gemstones have been valued for their rarity and their beauty. The most admired color for a ruby is a deep red. It's sometimes called "pigeon blood."

Materials:
"Gems & Jewels" Hands-on Handout (p. 25), large box of crayons, paper, pens or pencils, books about gemstones (see **Earth Resources**)

Directions:
1. Duplicate a copy of the "Gems & Jewels" handout and color according to the directions.
2. Show the children the pictures of the jewels on the sheet or in books. Review the names for the different jewels.
3. Divide the children into groups of four or five, and give each group an assortment of crayons from the crayon box.
4. Explain that the children's goal is to come up with ways to rename the colors. Someone who reads the new name should understand what the color is without having to see it.
5. Have the children color small areas on a piece of paper. They should label the colors A, B, C, and D. Below the colors, they should write their new color names. On the back of the paper, they should create an answer key.
6. Give the children an opportunity to walk around the room and try to match the colors with the new color names.
7. After everyone has had a chance to match the colors with the names, have the groups reveal the answers.
8. Children can vote on their favorite new color names.

Note:
Tourmalines and opals can come in many different colors.

Option:
• Do this activity with paint or fabric swatches.

Gems & Jewels

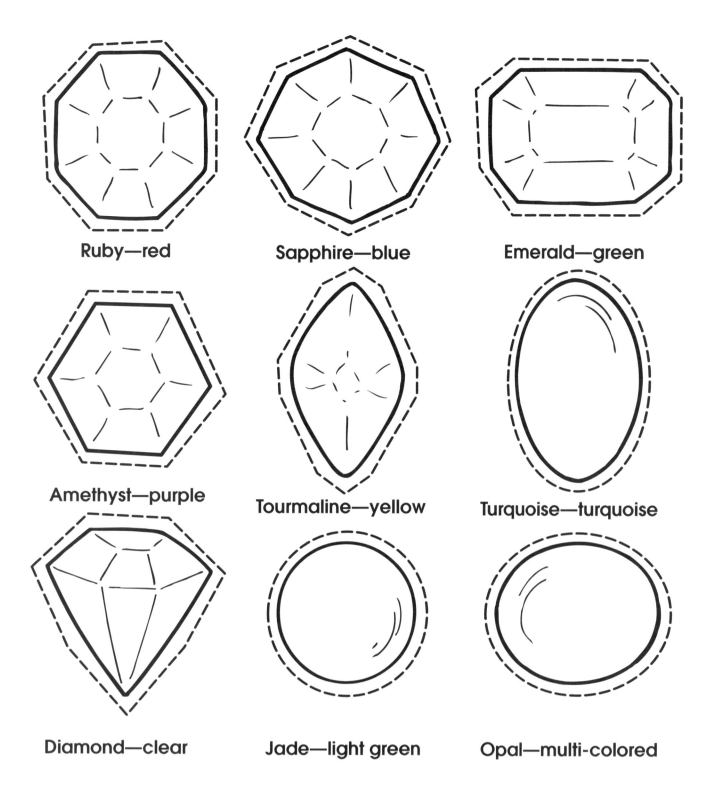

Ruby—red

Sapphire—blue

Emerald—green

Amethyst—purple

Tourmaline—yellow

Turquoise—turquoise

Diamond—clear

Jade—light green

Opal—multi-colored

Happy Earth Day!

Earth Day falls on April 22nd. However, you don't need a holiday to celebrate Mother Earth. Have the children create Earth awareness cards to exchange with each other or to give to their friends and families.

Materials:
Paper, crayons or markers, pens, construction paper, scissors, glue, glitter

Directions:
1. Explain that the children will be creating Earth-themed greeting cards.
2. Encourage the children to make their cards interesting. They might focus on environmental aspects, such as "Keep Earth Clean!" or they might choose to remind people about different Earth-related facts, such as "The Earth is the third planet from the sun."
3. Give each child a sheet of construction paper to fold into fourths. The children can then decorate the fronts of the cards and write messages inside the cards.
4. Display the cards before having the children either exchange them with each other or letting the children take the cards home to their families.

Option:
• Bring in several greeting cards for the children to observe before doing this activity. Many greeting cards are told in rhyme. The children might like to try their hand at creating rhyming cards.

Interview with an Explorer

Materials:
"Explorer Fact Sheet" Hands-on Handout (p. 28), "Explorer Interview Sheet" Hands-on Handout (p. 29), pencils or markers, "Super-Duper Fact Cards" (pp. 69-76)

Directions:
1. Have the children each choose an explorer to research. They can use the list below to get ideas. Explain that the children will be pretending to be the explorer they are researching.
2. Duplicate one copy of the "Explorer Fact Sheet" handout and the "Interview Sheet" for each child.
3. Have the children research the explorers using the guidelines on the "Explorer Interview Sheet" handout. They can use the "Super-Duper Fact Cards" at the end of the book, or they can use books from the library.
4. Once the children finish their research, divide them into pairs. Let each partner take a turn interviewing the other in front of the class.
5. Set up an interview schedule, perhaps working through five or six interviews per day.

Options:
• Children can dress up to look like their chosen explorers.
• Children can choose to interview spelunkers, geologists, or workers in other occupations that relate to the Earth.

Explorers to Research:
• Marco Polo: traveled to China
• Ferdinand Magellan: explored Straits of Magellan, Tierra del Fuego
• Henry Hudson: explored the Hudson River and Hudson Bay
• Juan Ponce de Leon: explored Florida
• James Cook: traveled through Bering Strait to Icy Cape, Alaska, and North Cape, Siberia
• Richard E. Byrd: established Little America on Bay of Whales
• Sacagawea: traveled westward with Lewis and Clark
• Cmdr. Finn Ronne & Mrs. H. Darlington: first women to winter on Antarctica

Explorer Fact Sheet

Use this fact sheet to record at least three facts about your chosen explorer. (Remember to list the books you used. If you use fact cards, write "fact card" under "Books I used.") You can use the back of this sheet if you need more space.

My name is: _____

My explorer is: _____

Fact: _____

_____

_____

Fact: _____

_____

_____

Fact: _____

_____

_____

Books I used:
Title: _____

Author: _____

Title: _____

Author: _____

Explorer Interview Sheet

Write your answers under the questions. Write your own question for question 5. Or use a new sheet of paper to write and answer all of your own questions. Your partner will use these questions to interview you in front of the class.

I am called a Viking.

Question 1: What country were you from?

_____

_____

Question 2: When did you live?

_____

_____

Question 3: What did you explore or discover?

_____

_____

Question 4: How did you travel?

_____

_____

Question 5:

_____

_____

Log of an Explorer

This is a fun activity in which the children pretend that they traveled with a famous explorer. They will learn facts about the explorer's journey and then write a log entry as if they were at the explorer's side. For instance, a child who chose to research Marco Polo might write about all of the different inventions he or she saw on the journey with Polo to China.

Materials:
Explorer's Log (p. 31), pens or pencils, crayons or markers, hole punch, yarn or brads, books on explorers (see **Earth Resources**)

Directions:
1. Have the children choose explorers to research. Encourage them to choose explorers different from the ones they picked for the "Interview with an Explorer" activity.
2. Provide assorted resources for the children to use for their research.
3. Have the children write brief reports as if they were members of the explorer's team. They should concentrate on the places they visited and the method of transportation they used.
4. Duplicate a copy of the Explorer's Log for each child.
5. Have the children copy their reports onto the log pattern. They should also draw a picture either of what they saw on their journeys or of the form of transportation they used.
6. Bind the completed log entries in a classroom "Explorers' Log" book.

Explorer's Log

Making a Mountain

Materials:
"What Makes a Mountain?" Hands-on Handout (p. 33), large sheet of butcher paper, tempera paint in assorted colors, shallow tins (for paint), paintbrushes, green tissue paper, glue, silver glitter

Directions:
1. Duplicate a copy of the "What Makes a Mountain?" Hands-on Handout for each child.
2. Explain that the children will be working together to make a representation of a Himalayan mountain.
3. Divide the children into five groups.
4. Give each group an assignment: tropical forests, leaf-shedding trees, cone-bearing evergreens, alpine meadows, or snow and ice all year.
5. Cut a large sheet of butcher paper. Then have the first group start at the bottom of the butcher paper and paint the tropical forest section of the mountain. When they're finished, the leaf-shedding trees group will paint their level, and so on up to the snow and ice group.
6. The children can use other art materials aside from paint to create their mountain levels. For instance, the tropical forest group can make three-dimensional trees from crumpled green tissue paper and the snow and ice group can sprinkle silver glitter onto their region.
7. Post the completed mountain on a wall in the classroom.

Option:
• Have the children research the different types of animals that can be found in various areas of Himalayan mountains. They can add these to their levels.

What Makes a Mountain?

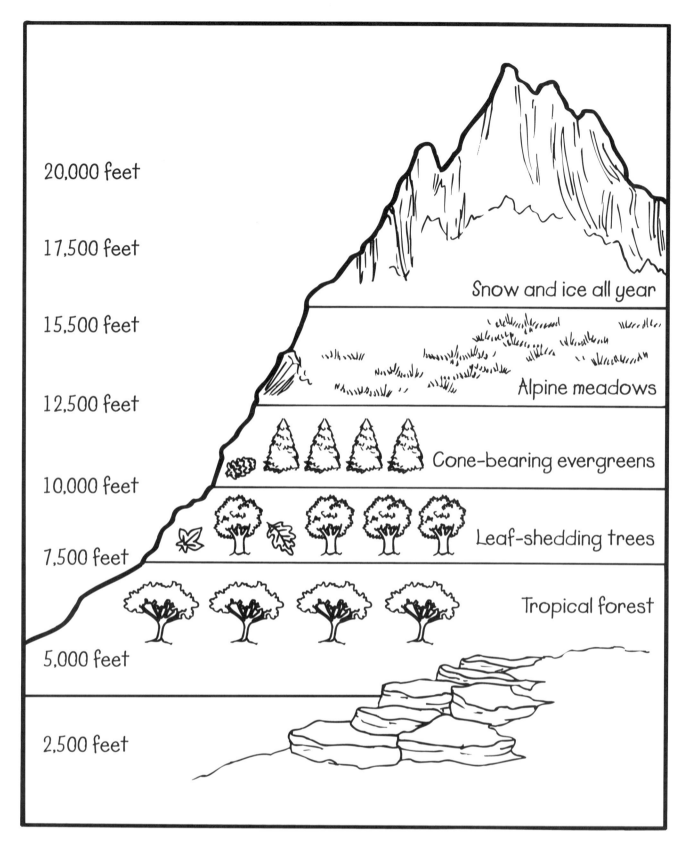

20,000 feet

17,500 feet

Snow and ice all year

15,500 feet

12,500 feet

Alpine meadows

Cone-bearing evergreens

10,000 feet

Leaf-shedding trees

7,500 feet

Tropical forest

5,000 feet

2,500 feet

Exciting Earth! © 2000 Monday Morning Books, Inc.

A Is for Avalanche

Materials:
"Earth A to Z List" (p. 77), "Super-Duper Fact Cards" (pp. 69-76), writing paper, drawing paper, heavy paper, pens or pencils, crayons or markers, hole punch, brads or yarn

Directions:
1. Explain that the children will be working together to create a classroom Earth ABC Book.
2. Have each child choose a topic to illustrate. They can choose from the "Earth A to Z List." Try to have one topic per letter of the alphabet. If there are more than 26 students in your class, you can feature more than one topic per letter. If you have fewer than 26 students, children could create pages for more than one letter.
3. Have the children research their chosen topic and write brief reports.
4. The children can illustrate their reports using crayons or markers
5. Make covers for the book using heavy paper. Then bind the completed pages in alphabetical order to create a classroom Earth ABC Book.
6. Share the ABC book with other classes.

Option:
• Have the children present their reports and pictures to the class in oral reports before binding the pages into the book.

Island Report Mural

This cooperative mural will reinforce the fact that there are islands all around the world. It will also introduce children to different types of islands.

Materials:
"Exploring Islands" Hands-on Handout (p. 36), construction paper, scissors, glue, butcher paper, blue tempera paint, shallow tins (for paint), pens or pencils, Island resources (see **Earth Resources**)

Directions:
1. Have the children name as many islands as they can think of. If they have trouble, refer to the list of islands below.
2. Explain that the children will each be researching an island. Let the children choose any islands they'd like.
3. Duplicate the "Exploring Islands" handout for each child. Children can use the questions as prompts for their research.
4. Provide a variety of resources for the children to use for research, including books, atlases, and encyclopedias.
5. Have the children cut island shapes from construction paper. They can try to cut their islands in the correct shapes by looking at maps or a globe.
6. Have the children write their reports on the island shapes.
7. Provide a large sheet of butcher paper for the children to paint blue for the background of the island reports.
8. The children can glue their reports to the dry mural.
9. Post the completed Island Report Mural on a wall.

Option:
• Cut pictures of islands from travel magazines or travel brochures to post in a border around the mural.

Islands:
• Inland Islands: Montreal, Isle Royale
• Coastal Islands: Long Island, Manhattan Island, Staten Island, the Florida Keys, the Scilly Isles
• Oceanic Islands: Hawaiian Islands, Galápagos Islands

Exploring Islands

My name is: _____

My island is: _____

1. Is your island an inland island, a coastal island, or an oceanic island?

_____

_____

_____

2. Islands are separated by water from other land areas. Sometimes they have unusual plants and animals. Does your island have any interesting creatures? If so, list them.

_____

_____

3. Sometimes islands have different climates than the nearby mainland. What type of weather does your island have?

_____

_____

4. Would you want to live on your island? Why or why not? (Use the back of this page.)

_____

_____

Creative Cave Report

Materials:
"Super-Duper Fact Cards" on caves (p. 69), stalactites (p. 74) and stalagmites (p. 75), Cave Dwellers (p. 38), sheet, clothesline, construction paper, scissors, glue, books about caves (see **Earth Resources**)

Directions:
1. Explain that the children will be creating a cooperative cave report.
2. Have each child choose a type of cave or an object or animal that can be found in a cave to research.
3. Provide a variety of sources, including the "Super-Duper Fact Cards," for the children to use to do their research.
4. Create a cave by stringing two lengths of clothesline across the classroom and draping a sheet over the line.
5. Have the children write their reports on pieces of paper cut to look like stalactites, stalagmites, or animals found in caves. Use the Cave Dwellers patterns, if desired.
6. Attach the reports to the cave using safety pins or clothespins attached to the clothesline. The stalactites should hang down from the top of the cave. Animals can be pinned directly to the sides of the cave. Stalagmites should be attached from the ground up.
7. Invite other classes to walk through the cave.

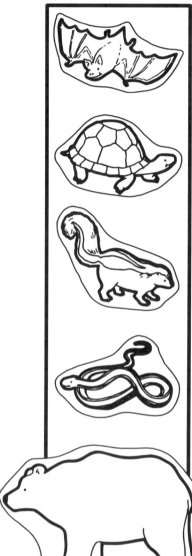

Options:
• Give each visitor an official spelunker's badge (p. 39). Fill in your room number in the space.
• Instead of creating a sheet cave, do this report as a wall mural.

Fun Fact:
• Some people once believed that caves were the homes of trolls.

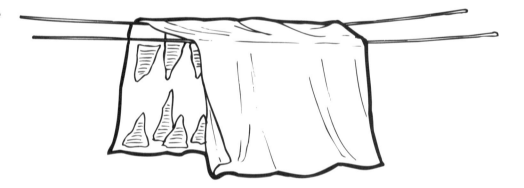

Cave Dwellers

Black bear

Box turtle

Bat

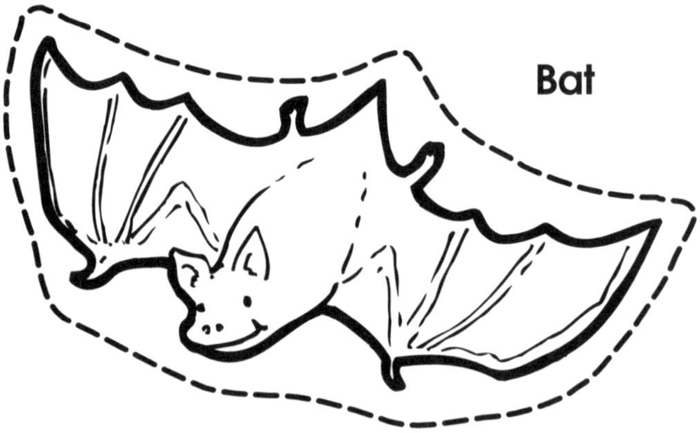

Skunk

Garter snake

Spelunker's Badges

_____
Name

I spelunked Class ____'s Cave!

_____
Name

I spelunked Class ____'s Cave!

_____
Name

I spelunked Class ____'s Cave!

_____
Name

I spelunked Class ____'s Cave!

_____
Name

I spelunked Class ____'s Cave!

_____
Name

I spelunked Class ____'s Cave!

_____
Name

I spelunked Class ____'s Cave!

_____
Name

I spelunked Class ____'s Cave!

Volatile Volcano Reports

These volatile reports erupt with fascinating facts about volcanoes.

Materials:
"Volcano Awareness" Hands-on Handout (p. 41), "Super-Duper Fact Card" on volcanoes (p. 76), Volcano (p. 52), large sheets of construction paper, pens, crayons or markers, scissors, glue, red and orange tempera paint, paintbrushes, shallow tins (for paint), red glitter, books about volcanoes (see **Earth Resources**)

Directions:
1. Duplicate a copy of the Volcano pattern for each child.
2. Explain that the children will be creating volcano reports.
3. Duplicate a copy of the "Volcano Awareness" handout and volcano "Super-Duper Fact Card" for children to use to do their research. They can also use books, encyclopedias, and the Web.
4. Have the children cut out the volcano pattern and glue it to a sheet of construction paper.
5. Have the children write their facts on the sheet of construction paper as if the facts were lava spewing from the volcano.
6. The children can add sparkle to their reports with red glitter, red and orange tempera paint, or other decorations.
7. Post the completed reports on a "Very Volatile Volcanoes" bulletin board.

Option:
• Have the children work on these reports together in groups.

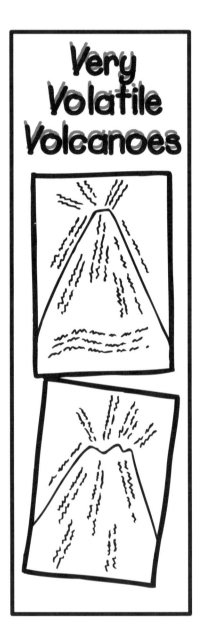

Volcano Awareness

There are four types of volcanoes.

Shield volcanoes have broad slopes. They look like an ancient soldier's shield. Mauna Loa and Kilauea are shield volcanoes

Cinder cone volcanoes look like upside-down ice cream cones.

Strato-volcanoes are made up of layers of ashes and cinders followed by layers of lava. Most volcanoes are strato-volcanoes. Mount Shasta is a strato-volcano.

Dome volcanoes have a steep dome shape. Mount St. Helens is a dome volcano.

Exciting Earth! © 2000 Monday Morning Books, Inc.

Exciting Environments

The Earth is made up of many different types of environments including deserts, tundras, wetlands, and rain forests.

Materials:
"Super-Duper Fact Cards" on deserts (p. 70), tundras (p. 75), rain forests (p. 73), and polar regions (p. 73), large sheets of construction paper, crayons or markers, books on various environments (see **Earth Resources**)

Directions:
1. Divide the children into small groups. Have each group choose one type of environment to research.
2. Have the children each learn at least three facts about their chosen areas.
3. Have the groups work together to create representations of their chosen environments. For instance, a group that chooses the desert would create a picture of a desert on a large sheet of construction paper.
4. Each child in the group should then add one fact to the picture. For example, in a desert picture, a child might write a fact about a cactus, or a desert-dwelling animal.
5. Post all of the completed picture reports on an "Exciting Environments" bulletin board.

Option:
• Challenge the children to find animals that live in their chosen regions. They can write their facts on drawings of the animals and then post them in the pictures. Or they can use the Animal Patterns (p. 43).

Exciting Earth! © 2000 Monday Morning Books, Inc.

Animal Patterns

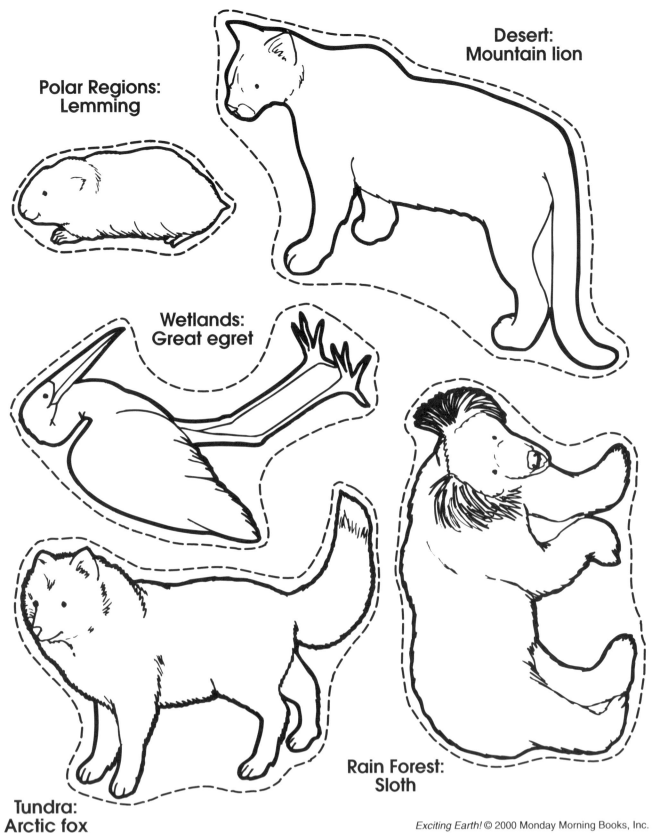

Polar Regions:
Lemming

Desert:
Mountain lion

Wetlands:
Great egret

Rain Forest:
Sloth

Tundra:
Arctic fox

Explaining Earth

Explorers have visited the far reaches of the Earth, from the polar regions to the exotic tropical islands. Your students will choose a part of the Earth to describe to an explorer from outer space.

Materials:
"Super-Duper Fact Cards" (pp. 69-76), writing paper, books about Earth (see **Earth Resources**)

Directions:
1. Have the children imagine that they have just met visitors who arrived on Earth from another planet. The visitors know nothing about planet Earth except for what they can see. What would the students want to tell them about Earth?
2. Have the children choose a part of Earth to explain to these imaginary visitors from outer space. They might describe their own town, or a specific Earth environment, such as a desert, forest, mountain, volcano, and so on. The children can use the "Super-Duper Fact Cards" or other resources to get ideas.
3. Give each child a sheet of writing paper.
4. Have the children write their descriptions of Earth for the imaginary visitors. They should describe the types of animals the visitors might come upon, which type of weather to expect, what plants the visitors might see, and so on.
5. Let the children share their reports with the class.

Exciting Earth! © 2000 Monday Morning Books, Inc.

Super Stone Quilt

Materials:
"Stone Facts" Hands-on Handout (p. 46), "Super-Duper Fact Card" on gemstones (p. 71), construction paper, colored tissue paper, glue, glitter, hole punch, yarn, additional gem and jewel resources (see **Earth Resources**)

Directions:
1. Explain that the children will be making a cooperative classroom quilt featuring different stones.
2. Have each child choose a stone to research. They can choose from those featured on the "Earth A to Z List," or from the "Stone Facts" handout, or they can research a stone of their choice. Children can focus on a specific type of gem, such as a diamond, or on one example of that stone, such as the Hope Diamond.
3. Provide assorted resources for the children to use.
4. Give each child a sheet of colored construction paper. Have the children use crumpled tissue paper to create three-dimensional stones. They can add sparkle with glitter.
5. Have the children write facts about their stones on the squares of construction paper.
6. Bind the quilt together by punching holes in all sides of the squares and tying with yarn. Add blank squares throughout the quilt to make even rows.
7. Hang the Super Stone quilt in the classroom or library where other students and faculty can enjoy it.

Option:
• If you live in an earthquake zone, make an earthquake quilt. Have each child make a square about earthquake preparedness.

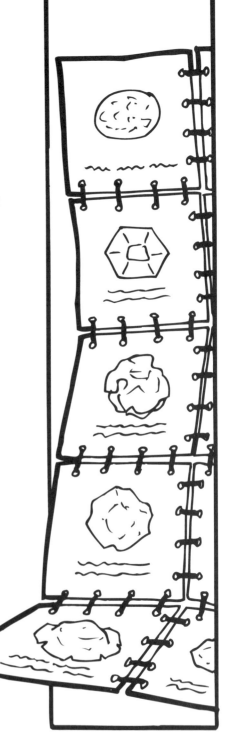

Stone Facts

Pumice is a type of lava rock filled with little holes. It is light enough to float on water. Pumice is the only rock that can float.

Diamonds can be colorless, brown, pink, green, and blue. Red diamonds are rare. Diamonds are the hardest known minerals.

Opals come in a range of different colors. The most precious opals are black opals.

Early people painted with dyes made by crushing rocks such as **malachite** (green), **hematite** (reddish-brown), and **chalk** (white).

Rubies are true red stones. Ruskin's Ruby in London's Natural History Museum is about 162 carats.

Emeralds are green gems. The finest emeralds in the world come from Colombia.

Tourmaline comes in many different colors. Watermelon tourmaline has a pink core with a green outside.

In the past, most **turquoise** was sold in Turkey. The word "turquoise" comes from a French term meaning "stone of Turkey."

Decorative stones include **turquoise**, **agate**, **jade**, and **lapis lazuli**.

Exciting Earth Glossary

Materials:
"Exciting Earth Glossary" Hands-on Handout (p. 48), dictionaries, pencils, construction paper, stapler, crayons or markers

Directions:
1. Duplicate one "Exciting Earth Glossary" Hands-on Handout for each child. Explain that a glossary is a list of special words with definitions listed after each word.
2. Have the children look up each word in the dictionary.
3. The children should write the definition next to the word to create their own glossaries. They can put the definitions into their own words. This will help them to remember the definitions later. Younger children can draw pictures to represent the meanings of the words.
4. As children learn new Earth words or phrases, they can add these to their glossaries.
5. Provide construction paper and a stapler for the children to use to bind their pages together. They can decorate the covers of the books with drawings of different landscapes.

Option:
• White-out the words on the "Exciting Earth Glossary" handouts and duplicate one page for each child. Let the children write in their own Earth words and definitions.

Exciting Earth Glossary

crust	
extinct	
geologist	
mantle	
stalactite	
stalagmite	
Spelunka	is the Latin word for cave

Volcanic Spelling Bee

Materials:
Lava Word Patterns (pp. 50-51), Volcano (p. 52),
crayons or markers, hat, scissors

Directions:
1. Duplicate the Lava Word Patterns, making one
sheet for each child and a few extra sheets for
teacher use.
2. Color the Volcano and post it on a bulletin board.
Cut out one extra set of lava words and post them
around the volcano, as if they were shooting out of
the top. (Cover the board before the spelling bee.)
3. Have the children learn how to spell each word.
(You might give the children the sheets to take
home and study at the beginning of the week, then
have the spelling bee at the end of the week.)
4. Host a spelling bee in your classroom. Keep one
set of lava words in a hat and pull out one at a
time, asking each child in turn to spell the word on
the piece of lava. (Older children may be able
to both spell and define the word.)
5. Continue with the spelling bee, having each child
who misspells a word sit down.

Note:
Choose words that are appropriate to your
children's spelling level. If a word is difficult for the
students, it could be classified as a bonus word. A
child who misspells it won't have to sit down, but
would get another turn with a different word.

Options:
• Duplicate blank pieces of lava and let children
write in their own Earth-related terms.
• Younger children can simply tape the lava words
to sheets of writing paper and practice copying
the words.

Exciting Earth! © 2000 Monday Morning Books, Inc.

Lava Word Patterns

Lava Word Patterns

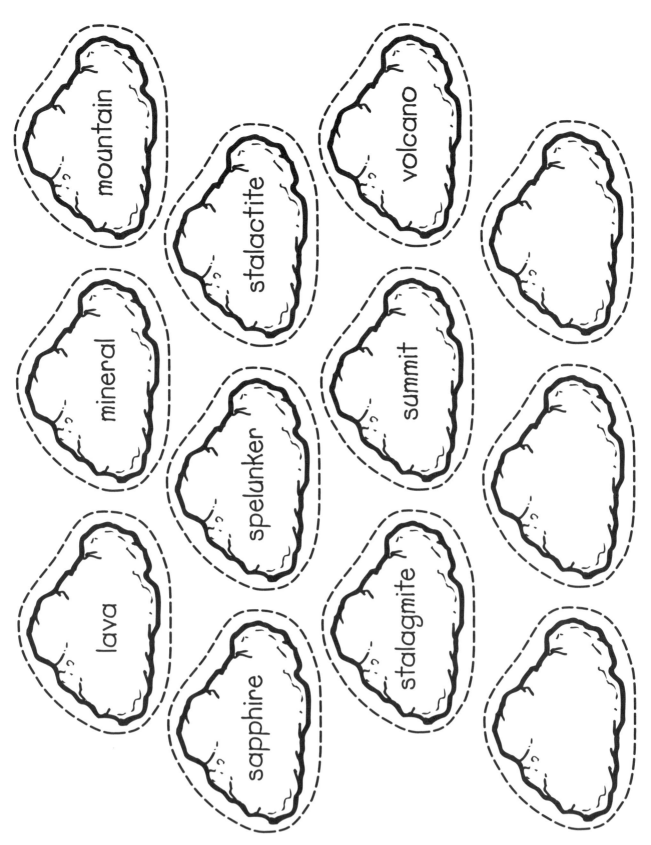

Volcano

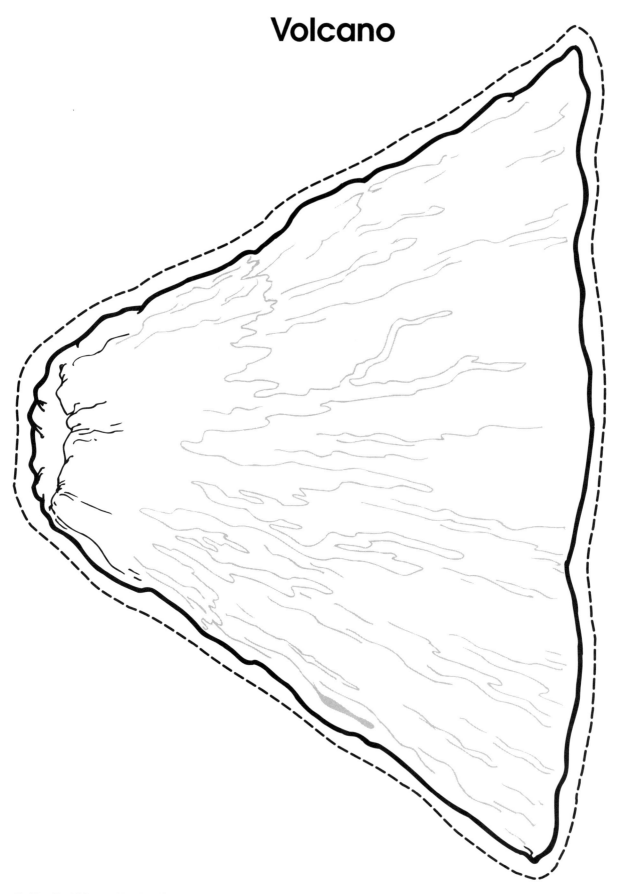

Create-a-Coin

Materials:
Construction paper, crayons or markers, pens or pencils, books on explorers (see **Earth Resources**)

Directions:
1. Explain that the young Shoshone woman named Sacagawea who helped adventurers Lewis and Clark is currently being honored with a dollar coin. If possible, show the children a picture of the coin on the U.S. Mint Web site.
2. Have the children each choose an explorer they believe should be honored with a coin.
3. Provide a variety of resources for the children to use to find representations of their chosen explorers.
4. Give each child a sheet of construction paper to cut into a coin shape.
5. Have the children draw a picture of their chosen explorers on the fronts of the coins. On the backs, the children should write facts about their chosen explorers.
6. Punch a hole in each coin and thread through with a piece of yarn.
7. Display the explorer coins by hanging them from the ceiling or from a piece of clothesline strung across the classroom. Observers can look at the pictures and read the facts.

U.S. Mint Web Site:
http://www.usmint.gov/dollarcoin/

The Island of the Skog

Story:
The Island of the Skog by Steven Kellogg (Dial, 1973).
A group of mice decide to sail away from the danger in
the city to find their own peaceful island. After quite a
while at sea, the mice find an island called the Island of
the Skog, population one Skog. The mice are afraid of
the Skog, since they don't know what a Skog is. The
Skog is afraid of the mice because they have set traps
for it. Luckily, after the group sorts out their
misunderstandings, the Skog and the mice
become friends.

Setting the Stage:
• Cut pictures of islands from travel brochures or travel
magazines, or ask for island posters from a local travel
agency. Post the pictures in the classroom.
• Read the children the chapter book *Surprise Island* by
Gertrude Chandler Warner.
• Display a variety of mice books around the classroom,
such as *The Tailor of Gloucester* by Beatrix Potter,
Chrysanthemum, *Owen*, or *Julius: The Baby of the World*
by Kevin Henkes.
• Have the children exchange plastic leis in the tradition
of the islands of Hawaii.

Tricky Tongue Twister:
Mice pay twice the price for rice.

The Island Rhyme

This activity will bring out the poet in your students. Before beginning the activity, consider sharing an assortment of poetry books with the children, including *Now We Are Six* and *When We Were Very Young* by A. A. Milne, any of Dr. Seuss' rhyming books, and *Where the Sidewalk Ends* by Shel Silverstein.

Materials:
Paper, pencils or pens, crayons or markers

Directions:
1. At the end of *The Island of the Skog* is a poem that the mice and the Skog sing together. Read this poem several times to the children.
2. Explain that the children will be writing their own island poems. They can base the poems on the story *The Island of the Skog*, or they can write the poems about island facts they've learned during the Earth unit.
3. Have the children study a poem, either the one in *The Island of the Skog* or one from a book you've brought into the classroom. Point out how the rhyme scheme works. For instance, in the poem in *The Island of the Skog*, the first and second lines rhyme, the third and fourth lines rhyme, and so on. Some poems rhyme the first and third lines. Start the children off with rhymes of either two lines or four lines.
4. Have the children think about what they want to say. Then they should look for words that they can make rhyme.
5. Let the children share their poems with the rest of the class. They can illustrate the poems first, if they'd like.

Option:
• Start the children off by having them rewrite a poem, such as "Roses Are Red." New words or phrases can easily be inserted into this poem, such as: *Islands are green, the sky is blue, I need a vacation, and so do you*! The children can keep the ending words the same.

Ming Lo Moves the Mountain

Story:
Ming Lo Moves the Mountain by Arnold Lobel (Greenwillow, 1982).
In this magical story, Ming Lo and his wife live in the shadow of a great mountain. Stones and rocks fall from the mountain and pierce holes in their roof. The wife decides that the mountain must be moved, so Ming Lo goes to a wise man for help. The wise man makes several suggestions for ways that Ming Lo and his wife might move the mountain. Finally, the wise man comes up with the dance of the moving mountain. To the great delight of Ming Lo and his wife, the dance works.

Setting the Stage:
• Post pictures of mountains around the room. Cut them from colorful construction paper, or cut pictures from travel magazines or brochures.
• Serve cakes and bread like the ones Ming Lo and his wife made to appease the spirit of the mountain.
• Take the children on a hike if there are mountains near you.
• Read the children the chapter book *Mountain Top Mystery* by Gertrude Chandler Warner.
• Have the children create their own dance of the moving mountain. Do this outdoors where the children have plenty of room to move. Once the children have created their dances, let them share the dances with the rest of the class.

Tricky Tongue Twister:
Count the fountains on the mountain.

How I'd Move a Mountain

After reading *Ming Lo Moves the Mountain*, discuss problem-solving with the children. The wise man in the story offers several solutions to Ming Lo's problem. Finally, the wise man offers a suggestion that works.

Materials:
Paper, pencils, crayons or markers

Directions:
1. Ask the children to think about the way the wise man solved Ming Lo's problems in *Ming Lo Moves the Mountain*.
2. Have the children put themselves in the position of the wise man in the story. (They will be wise men and wise women.)
3. Give each child a piece of paper, a pencil, and crayons or markers. Have the children think of how they might have solved the problem if Ming Lo had come to them for help.
4. Once the children have written and illustrated their ideas, let them share their ideas with the class.
5. The class can vote on their favorite ways to move the mountain.

Options:
• The children can work together in small groups to come up with mountain-moving suggestions.
• Have the children write their problem-solving suggestions on papers cut to look like mountains. Post the completed papers in a mountain range format on a bulletin board.

Exciting Earth! © 2000 Monday Morning Books, Inc.

The Magic School Bus Inside the Earth

Story:
The Magic School Bus Inside the Earth by Joanna Cole & Bruce Degen (Scholastic, 1987).
Ms. Frizzle's class is studying the Earth. Each child must bring a rock to school as part of a homework assignment. When only four children complete the assignment, Ms. Frizzle takes the class on a field trip to collect rocks. On this exciting field trip, the class winds up first in the center of the Earth, and then on a volcanic island, before finally ending up back at their school.

Setting the Stage:
• Take the children on a field trip to a museum where they can observe a rock collection.
• Invite a geologist to talk to the children about different types of rocks.
• Let any children who collect rocks bring their collection in to share.
• Show the children one of the episodes from *The Magic School Bus* television series. Videotapes are often available at libraries.
• Read *Everybody Needs a Rock* by Byrd Baylor, illustrated by Peter Parnall (Scribner's Sons, 1974). This interesting book lists ten fascinating rules for finding the perfect rock. Read it to the children. Then let them go rock hunting!

Tricky Tongue Twisters:
• *Did you see? She sells shale.*
• *Observe obsidian. See slate.*

Our Class Rode The Magic School Bus

Materials:
School Bus (p. 60), pens or pencils, scissors

Directions:
1. Duplicate a copy of the School Bus for each child. Cut them out.

2. After reading *The Magic School Bus inside the Earth*, have the children imagine that their class was going to ride the magic bus.

3. Give each child a bus. On the school bus-shaped papers, have the children write down an imaginary trip that their own class took on the Magic School Bus. They can feature you in Ms. Frizzle's spot.

4. Post the completed stories on a "Magic School Bus" bulletin board.

Options:
• Display other episodes in *The Magic School Bus* series below the bulletin board.

• Have the children write about a real field trip that your class took.

• Duplicate the buses on light yellow paper.

School Bus

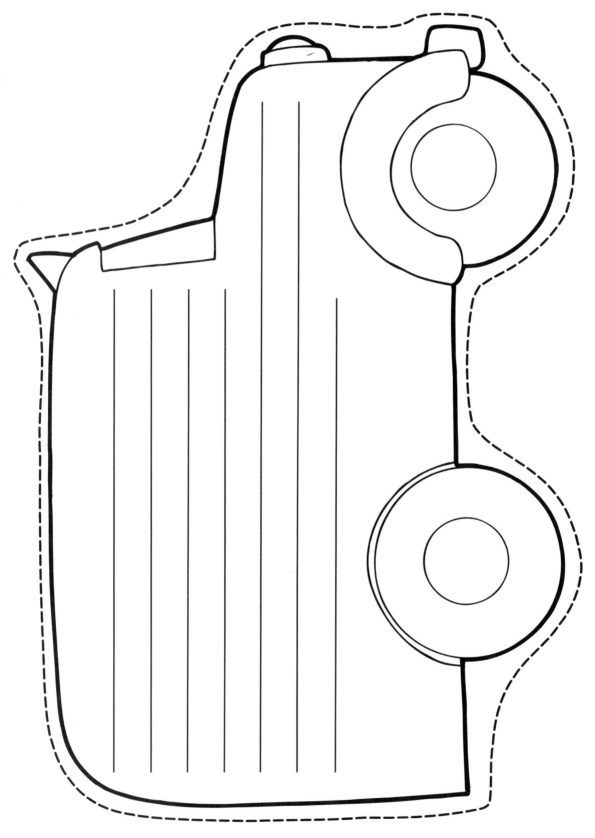

The Little Prince

Story:
The Little Prince by Antoine de Saint Exupéry, translated by Katherine Woods (Harcourt Brace Jovanovich, 1943, 1971).

This fairy tale is about a little prince who comes from another planet. The Little Prince's planet is no larger than a house. It has three volcanoes, two active and one extinct. The Little Prince also owns a flower that is unlike any other flower in the galaxy. In this story, the Little Prince visits a variety of planets inhabited by different types of people.

Setting the Stage:
• Post pictures of the planets around the room. You can use the Planetary Patterns (p. 9).
• Play French music to the children, or teach them "Alouette." (*The Little Prince* was originally written in French.)
• Bring in a passport for the children to see. The Little Prince travels from planet to planet without a passport, but if the children were traveling from country to country, they would need one.
• Cut beautiful flowers from gardening catalogs to use to decorate the room.

Tricky Tongue Twister:
The prince plays planetary polka.

Exciting Earth! © 2000 Monday Morning Books, Inc.

My Little Planet

The students live on Earth, the third planet from the sun. However, in this assignment, they will pretend that they each have their own planets. The children can use what they've learned about planet Earth in the descriptions of their planets. For instance, they can give their planets mountains, earthquakes, volcanoes, avalanches, and so on.

Materials:
Construction paper, scissors, pens or pencils, glitter, glue, assorted decorations

Directions:
1. Have the children imagine that they live on their own planets. They should think about the size of their planets and what their planets look like.
2. Provide construction paper, crayons or markers, and assorted decorations for the children to use to create replicas of their planets.
3. Have the children write descriptions of their planets. How large are they and where are they in relation to the sun and Earth?
4. Have the children name their planets.
5. Post the completed planet pictures and descriptions on a bulletin board labeled "Out of This World!"

Options:
• The children can describe the type of plants and animals that live on their planets.
• The children can write imaginary stories of what a day is like on their planets. Is there sunlight? Do their planets have more than one moon?

Exciting Earth Program

Songs:
- An Earthquake's Scary
- If I Had a Mountain
- In an Earthquake
- In a Cavern, In a Canyon
- Amethysts, Diamonds, Emeralds
- Hillary, Frobisher, Smith, and Captain Cook

Featuring:

An Earthquake's Scary

(to the tune of "My Bonnie Lies Over the Ocean")

An earthquake's a scary adventure,
The ground moves right under your feet.
Plates fall and the windows start shaking,
And cracks sometimes form in the street,
    the street.
Don't go outside in an earthquake,
Get under your desk, your desk.
Don't go outside in an earthquake,
Get under your desk!

If I Had a Mountain

(to the tune of "If I Had a Hammer")

If I had a mountain,
I'd climb it in the morning,
I'd climb it in the evening,
To look at the land.
I'd climb it in summer,
I'd climb it in winter,
I'd climb it in the fall and spring,
The daytime and nighttime,
And I'd look at the land.

In an Earthquake

(to the tune of "Clementine")

In an earthquake, don't you panic,
Just stay calm and keep your head.
If inside, stand in a corner,
Or get underneath your desk.

If you're outside, in an earthquake,
Stay away from trees and poles,
Don't go near buildings or cables,
Any structures that might fall.

If you're in a crowded building,
Don't go run across the floor,
It's much safer to stay calm,
And not go rushing for the door.

Exciting Earth! © 2000 Monday Morning Books, Inc.

In a Cavern, In a Canyon

(to the tune of "Clementine")

In a cavern, in a canyon,
Things are growing all around.
A stalactite's on the ceiling
A stalagmite's on the ground.

There are glow worms
In New Zealand
That make caves look very bright,
In the darkness of the cavern,
They appear like stars at night.

There are tunnels made in glaciers,
Some volcanoes can make caves.
There are caverns made of limestone,
And sea caves are made by waves.

In a cavern, in a canyon,
A stalagmite's on the ground.
A stalactite's on the ceiling,
Things are growing all around.

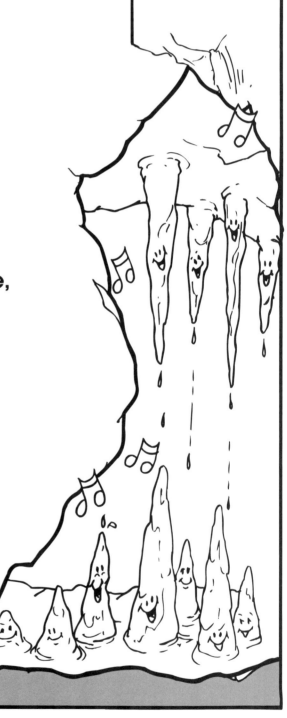

Amethysts, Diamonds, Emeralds

(to the tune of "Jingle Bells")

Amethysts, diamonds,
Emeralds so green
Tourmalines and turquoise
With a pretty sheen.
Sapphires and opals,
Shine with all their might.
So many different gemstones
That twinkle in the light.

Oh, sapphires are blue,
And emeralds are green,
Turquoise is blue, too,
But not the tourmalines.

Opals have a glow,
Like fire burning bright,
And amber is yellow,
While much of quartz is white.

Oh, amethysts, diamonds,
Emeralds so green
Tourmalines and turquoise
With a pretty sheen.
Sapphires and opals,
Shine with all their might.
So many different gemstones
That twinkle in the light.

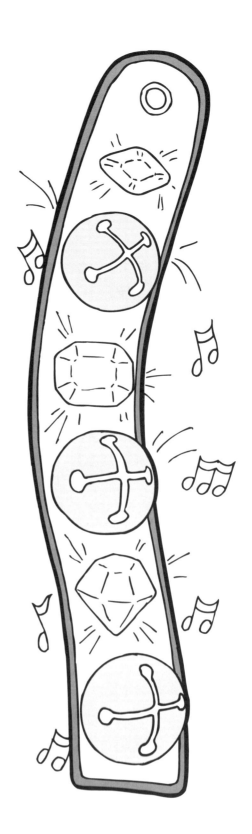

Hillary, Frobisher, Smith, and Captain Cook

(to the tune of "Jingle Bells")

Hillary, Frobisher, Smith, and Captain Cook,
Clark and Marco Polo, but not Captain Hook,
Christopher Columbus, Drake, and Admiral Byrd,
They all were famed explorers,
Who traveled 'round the world.

On elephants and boats,
They charted land and sea,
Explorers wrote the maps,
That help both you and me.

On camels and on foot,
Cross mountains and the sand,
Explorers worked so hard,
To tame this wild land.

Oh, Hillary, Frobisher, Smith, and Captain Cook,
Clark and Marco Polo, but not Captain Hook,
Christopher Columbus, Drake, and Admiral Byrd,
They all were famed explorers,
Who traveled 'round the world.

Cave and Cavern Facts

Locations: Caves and caverns exist in many parts of the world.
Age: Some are millions of years old.
Experts: Speleologists are experts who know a lot about caves. Spelunkers are people who explore caves.
Formation: There are sea caves, ice caves, volcanic caves, and limestone caves.
Super-Duper Fact: Glow worms in New Zealand's Waitomo Cave look like stars in the night sky.

Christopher Columbus Facts

Location: Christopher Columbus was born in 1451 in Genoa, Italy.
Occupation: Columbus first was a sailor. Then he ran a shop with his brother. They sold books.
Traveler: In 1492, Spain's king and queen gave Columbus three ships: the Niña, the Pinta, and the Santa María.
Super-Duper Fact: When Columbus landed in America, he thought he had reached the Indies. This is why he named the natives he met Indians.

Desert Facts

Animals: Deserts can be homes to mountain lions, spadefoot toads, bats, foxes, sheep, birds, reptiles, and insects.
Plants: Some deserts have night-blooming flowers that open after dark.
Water: Deserts can get water from rain and from melted snow.

Super-Duper Fact: A saguaro cactus may grow to be 50 feet (15 m) tall!

Earthquake Facts

Location: Most earthquakes happen in the Earth's crust.
How they happen: Cracks in the rocks run through the crust. The two sides push against each other. Then the rocks move past each other.
Description: Any vibration in the Earth's crust is an earthquake.

Small shakers: Most earthquakes are too small to be felt. Scientists use sensitive instruments to study them.
Super-Duper Fact: There are about one million quakes every year.

Gemstone Facts

Different types: Gemstones include opals, diamonds, emeralds, rubies, and sapphires.
Made of: All gemstones are minerals. Minerals are nonliving solids found in nature.
Artsy: Gemstones are often used in jewelry making and in art.

Super-Duper Fact: The Hope Diamond has a bad reputation. People believe that it brings bad luck. It is 45.52 carats and is now in the Smithsonian Institution in Washington, D.C.

Island Facts

Three types: Inland islands are in rivers and lakes. Oceanic islands are far from the continents. Coastal islands are closer to the continents.
Made of: Most oceanic islands are volcanic. It can take millions of years before the sea-floor volcano reaches the surface to become an island.

Super-Duper Fact: Montreal, a city in Canada, is built on a long river island.

Exciting Earth! © 2000 Monday Morning Books, Inc.

Mountain Facts

Description: Most mountains are part of chains or ranges.
Creation: When the Earth's plates push and pull against each other, this can create mountain ranges.
Helpful mountains: Many farms and cities rely on mountain lakes for drinking water.

Super-Duper Fact: The tallest mountain is Mount Everest. It is 29,028 feet (8,848 m) above sea level. Eight of the world's ten highest mountains are in Nepal.

Marco Polo Facts

Traveler: Marco Polo traveled from Venice to China in 1271. He was 17 years old.
Inventions: In China, Polo saw amazing inventions, including kites, gunpowder, printing, umbrellas, spaghetti, paper, a compass, and a spinning wheel.
Occupation: In China, the Kublai Khan made Polo the governor of Kinsai, the most civilized city in the world.
Super-Duper Fact: Marco Polo traveled for 24 years. He returned to Venice at 41.

Rain Forest Facts

Animals: Many mammals, birds, reptiles, and amphibians live in rain forests, from tiny mites to giant jaguars.

Wet weather: Rain falls nearly every day in tropical rain forests. There is usually at least 60 in (152 cm) of rain per year, and often there's even more than that.

Super-Duper Fact: Rain forest trees can be 200 ft (60 m) tall. These trees tower over the top of the rain forest, which is called the canopy.

Polar Region Facts

Where: The polar regions are at the top and the bottom of the world.

Animals: Different animals are found at the different poles. Emperor penguins live in the cold areas south of the Antarctic circle. Lemmings live in the Arctic circle.

Super-Duper Fact: Explorers didn't go to the North and South poles until the first part of the 20th century.

Exciting Earth! © 2000 Monday Morning Books, Inc.

Sacagawea Facts

Lifetime: Sacagawea, a young Shoshone woman, was born around 1789.
Marriage: She was married to a French-Canadian fur trapper.
Known for: She helped blaze a trail into uncharted land.
Traveler: She traveled with Lewis and Clark. Her job was to serve as a guide, find food, and work as an interpreter.
Super-Duper Fact: Sacagawea brought her baby with her.

Stalactite Facts

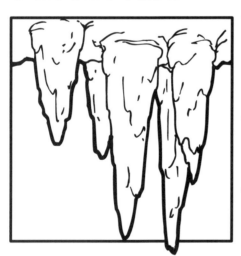

What it is: A stalactite is a rock formation that hangs from the ceiling of a cave.
How they form: Stalactites start with a drop of water on a cave ceiling. The water drop contains dissolved limestone. Each drop trickling through the growing ring of stone adds another layer.
Mnemonic: Stala**c**tites hang down from the **c**eiling.
Super-Duper Fact: Most stalactites grow only about .5 in (1.27 cm) in 100 years!

Stalagmite Facts

What it is: A stalagmite is a rock formation that grows slowly up from a cave floor.
How they form: Stalagmites grow from the ground up when drops of water containing dissolved limestone drip to the cave's floor.
Mnemonic: Remember that stalagmites **g**row from the **g**round up.
Super-Duper Fact: Stalagmites can grow to be more than 45 feet tall and 30 feet wide.

Tundra Facts

Formation: Tundra is formed by extreme cold and nearly constant wind.
Where it is: Tundra covers more than 9 million sq. miles (23 million sq. km.) of the Earth's surface.
Types: There are two types of tundra: Arctic and Alpine.
Animals: Lemmings, ground squirrels, Arctic hares, foxes, wolves, musk oxen, and grizzly bears live on the tundra.
Super-Duper Fact: "Tundra" means "marshy plain" and "land of no trees."

Volcano Facts

Extinct: Extinct volcanoes no longer erupt.
Location: The Earth's crust is broken into huge sections called plates. Most volcanoes erupt where two plates meet.
Helpful: Volcanoes help create mountains, islands, and new soil.
Average: Each year, about 20 to 30 volcanoes erupt.
Underwater: Some underwater volcanoes rise from the ocean floor as islands.
Super-Duper Fact: More than 600 volcanoes are active.

Wetland Facts

Area: Wetlands cover 6 percent of the Earth's total land area.
Location: Any low point of land that collects water may support a wetland. These include the edges of rivers and lakes.
Common types: Freshwater marshes and swamps are the two most common wetlands.
Super-Duper Fact: A variety of animals live in wetlands, including turtles, frogs, birds, bobcats, moose, rabbits, deer, snakes, and alligators.

Earth A to Z List

A: Avalanche
B: Basalt, Beryl
C: Cinnabar, Crust
D: Desert, Diamond, Dome Volcanoes
E: Emerald, Everest
F: Fujiyama, Feldspar
G: Garnet, Geologist, Glacier, Granite
H: Hematite
I: Island
J: Jade
K: Kilimanjaro
L: Lava, Limestone Caves
M: Marble, Matterhorn, Minerals, Mountains
N: North Pole
O: Obsidian, Olympus, Opal
P: Pangaea, Pikes Peak, Pumice
Q: Quartz
R: Ruby
S: Shale, Spelunker, Stalactite, Stalagmite, Sulfur
T: Topaz, Tundra, Turquoise
U: Ural
V: Vesuvius, Volcano
W: Waitomo Cave, Wetlands
X: Xizang
Y: Yukon
Z: Zircon

Exciting Earth! © 2000 Monday Morning Books, Inc.

Earth Resources

Avalanches:
• *Avalanche* by Michael J. Rosen, illustrated by David Butler.

Caves and Caverns:
• *Caves* by Stephen Kramer, photographs by Kenrick L. Day (Carolrhoda, 1995).
• *Caves and Caverns* by Gail Gibbons (Harcourt Brace, 1993).
• *One Small Square Cave* by Donald M. Silver, illustrated by Patricia J. Wynne (W. H. Freeman, 1993).

Deserts:
• *A Living Desert* by Guy J. Spencer, photographs by Tim Fuller (Troll, 1988).

Earth:
• *Jigsaw Continents* by Melvin Berger, illustrated by Bob Totten (Coward, McCann & Geoghegan, 1977).
• *Mission Earth: Voyage to the Home Planet* by June A. English and Thomas D. Jones (Scholastic, 1996).
• *Planet Earth* by Christopher Lampton (Franklin Watts, 1982).
• *Planet Earth/Inside Out* by Gail Gibbons (Morrow, 1995).

Earthquakes:
• *Earthquake* by Christopher Lampton (Millbrook, 1991).
• *Earthquakes* by Seymour Simon (Morrow, 1991).

Explorers:
• *The Adventures of Marco Polo* by Demi (Holt, Rinehart and Winston, 1982).
• *Amerigo Vespucci: Scientist and Sailor* by Ronald Syme, illustrated by William Stobbs (William Morrow, 1969).
• *Edmund Hillary* by Timothy R. Gaffney (Childrens Press, 1990).

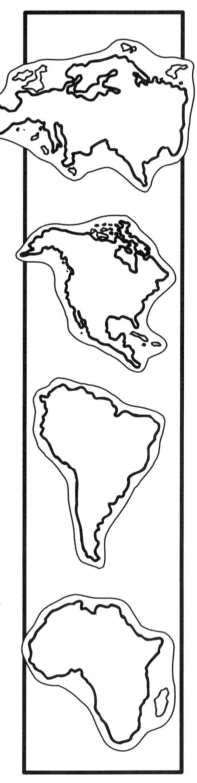

Earth Resources

Explorers:
• *Henry Hudson: Arctic Explorer and North American Adventurer*
by Isaac Asimov and Elizabeth Kaplan (Gareth Stevens, 1991).
• *Juan Ponce de León* by Sean Dolan (Chelsea House, 1995).
• *A Picture Book of Christopher Columbus* by David A. Adler,
illustrated by John & Alexandra Wallner (Holiday House, 1991).
• *Marco Polo* by Gian Paolo Ceserani, illustrated
by Piero Ventura (Putnam's Sons, 1977).
• *Sacagawea: Indian Interpreter to Lewis and Clark*
by Marion Marsh Brown (Childrens Press, 1988).
• *Sacagawea: Westward with Lewis and Clark*
by Alana J. White (Enslow, 1997).

Gems & Jewels:
• *Crystal & Gem* by Dr. R. F. Symes and Dr. R. R. Harding
(Knopf, 1991).
• *Rocks & Minerals* by Dr. R. F. Symes and the staff of the
Natural History Museum, London (Knopf, 1988).

Islands:
• *Islands* by William M. Stephens, illustrated by Lydia Rosier
(Holiday House, 1974).

Mountains:
• *Mountains* by Philip Sauvain (Carolrhoda, 1996).
• *Mountains* by Seymour Simon (Morrow, 1994).

Polar Regions:
• *Animals of the Polar Regions* by Sylvia A. Johnson,
illustrated by Alcuin C. Dornisch (Lerner, 1976).

Rain Forests:
• *Conserving Rain Forests* by Martin Banks (Steck-Vaughn, 1989).
• *Explore the World of Exotic Rainforests* by Anita Ganeri
(Ilex, 1992).
• *Journey Through a Tropical Jungle* by Adrian Forsyth (Simon &
Schuster, 1988).
• *Jungle* by Theresa Greenaway (Dorling Kindersley, 1994).

Earth Resources

Rain Forests:
• *The Most Beautiful Roof in the World: Exploring the Rainforest Canopy* by Kathryn Lasky, photographs by Christopher G. Knight (Harcourt Brace, 1997).
• *Nature's Green Umbrella: Tropical Rain Forests* by Gail Gibbons (Morrow, 1994).
• *One Day in the Tropical Rain Forest* by Jean Craighead George (Thomas Y. Crowell, 1990).
• *Rain Forest* by Barbara Taylor (Dorling Kindersley, 1991).
• *Rain Forest Babies* by Kathy Darling (Walker, 1996).

Volcanoes:
• *Volcanoes* by Peter Murray (The Child's World, 1996).
• *Volcanoes* by Seymour Simon (Morrow, 1988).

Wetlands:
• *America's Wetlands* by Frank Staub (Carolrhoda, 1995).

Tundra:
• *Tundra* by Donna Walsh Shepherd (Franklin Watts, 1996).

Caves and Caverns to Visit:
• Carlsbad Caverns, Carlsbad, New Mexico
• Howe Caverns, Howes Cave, New York
• Luray Caverns, Luray, Virginia
• Mammoth Cave, Mammoth Cave National Park, Kentucky
• Onondaga Cave, Leesburg, Missouri
• Waitomo Cave, New Zealand